CLARA BECOMES A CITIZEN

by Evelyn Rothstein

Illustrated by Elizabeth Uhlig

MARBLE HOUSE EDITIONS

Published by Marble House Editions
96-09 66th Avenue (Suite 1D)
Rego Park, NY 11374

Library of Congress Cataloguing-in-Publication
Data
Rothstein, Evelyn
Clara Becomes a Citizen/by Evelyn Rothstein

Summary: A Russian woman living in the U.S. in
the 1930s longs to pass the citizenship test, and is
coached by her school-age daughter.

ISBN 0-9786745-7-X
Library of Congress Catalog Card Number 2009921179

Printed in China

To Charmion Lord, friend and citizen, and
to all Americans who have the inalienable right to
become and be voting citizens, without barriers to
gender, color, race, or disability.

This story which our Grandma Evelyn told us is about our Great Grandma Clara. We would like to share this story because it tells so much about what life was like a long time ago when Clara came to America and wished to become an American citizen. It is also about how life is today, when so many immigrants want the opportunity to become American citizens.

Tyler, Eliza, Abigail, Margo, Jane

TABLE OF CONTENTS

CHAPTER ONE – 1920

I was already seventeen years old when I came from Europe to America. I could read and write Yiddish, but I knew almost nothing in English. And because Yiddish is written with Hebrew letters, I didn't even know how to read the English alphabet. But I knew I had to learn to speak and read and write English.

When I got to America, I moved in with my Aunt Rose and got a job sewing dresses in a factory.

"You must also go to night school," Aunt Rose told me.

Night schools were where immigrants went to learn English. They came to America from Italy, Poland, Hungary, Russia, Czechoslovakia, and other countries, and would attend night school after work.

Going to night school was difficult because my day was so long. I would take the subway to the factory at 8:00 in the morning and work till 6:00 at night. Then I would ride the subway home, eat fast, and run off to the school, which was about ten blocks from my house. I was often tired and would try not to fall asleep in class.

Learning English was hard. None of the words sounded like they did in Yiddish. We had to read the English letters, which go from left to right, not like Yiddish, which goes from right to left.

Everyone in the class made mistakes. Sometimes the teacher wasn't patient, and he would laugh when he heard our accents or when we said something he thought sounded funny.

Most of the time I didn't understand what he was saying. Even worse was that I couldn't understand what the *other* people in the class were saying. And even *more* terrible was that people in the class didn't understand what *I* was saying.

I would go home and wish that people in America spoke Yiddish. But that was impossible. And people from Italy were probably wishing that everyone spoke Italian. But people in America spoke *English*! So no matter how tired I was after work, I always went to night school.

Aa Bb Cc Dd Ee Ff Gg Hh Ii

- Hello!
- How do you do?
- ... ne, thank you,
    and you?
- My name is ___

Little by little, I began to understand what people were saying, and soon I could even answer them, especially people in the food stores.

"How are you today, Clara?"

"I'm good," I would answer.

"What can I get for you today? We have fresh tomatoes, peaches, sweet plums."

"These," and I would point to the peaches. "Just two," and I would show two fingers.

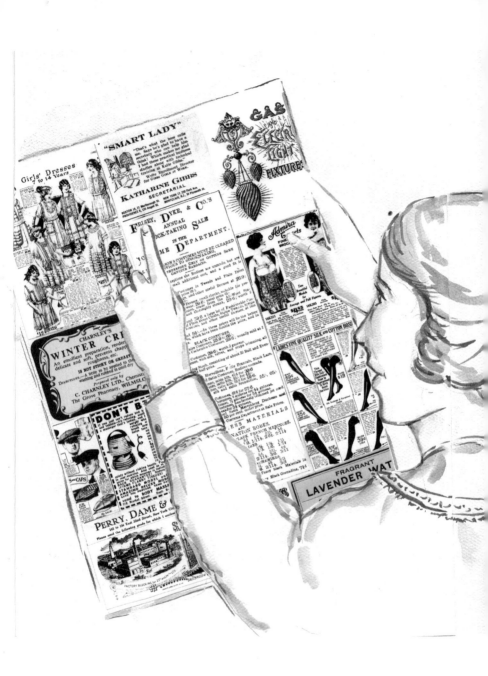

About a year later, I could tell that my English was getting better. Every day when I went to work, I would buy a newspaper and read the headlines or the ads for dresses.

My younger sister Sylvia was able to go to regular school, so at night she would show me her schoolbooks and teach me how to read the easy words.

I could now go into a clothing store and start talking to the person selling.

"I want a dress like the one in the window."

"How about this one?" the saleswoman would ask.

"No. Not so good a color. I don't think it fit me. What else you have? Maybe one with belt and maybe nice buttons. One good for a party and also for work too, when we have special day."

Two years after I was in America, I could
speak English with all the people in the
factory who didn't know Yiddish. Filomena
Domenica, who was from Italy, spoke with
a funny Italian accent, and I spoke back to
her with a funny Yiddish accent. But we
understood what we were saying, and we
could laugh at each other's English.

CHAPTER TWO – 1925 - 1926

When I had been in America for five years, I began to think that I should become an American citizen. I would then be able to vote for the president of the United States and the mayor of New York City. The teacher in night school would point his finger at us and say, "To be a good American you must vote, and to vote you must be a citizen. Every immigrant who comes to America should become a citizen."

But to become an American citizen I would have to pass a test, a test in English and a test with questions about American history. I wasn't so worried anymore about English, although I read very slowly. But I was really scared about the other test. My friends had told me that it was all about American history and I hardly knew anything. Jenny, a friend of mine who came to America when she was nine years old, told me, "Don't even try to take the test. They'll ask you all about the presidents, every single one, and how many years they were president, and what they did, and more. Don't even try."

I went to the public library and asked the librarian for an easy book on American history. She pointed to the shelves that said *American History*. There were lots and lots of books and every one was thick and heavy. I took one off the shelf, looked inside it and tried to read the first chapter, "The Discovery of America." I could hardly understand the words. I skipped to the next chapter – "The Early Settlements." That one had more hard words with lots of names of people and places I had never heard of. *Isn't there an easy history book?* I wondered.

~Library Rules~
1. NO SHOUTING
2. DO NOT PUT BOOKS BACK.
3. BE COURTEOUS
4. NO LOITERING

I took out a book anyway and hoped Sylvia could help me. But even though Sylvia was a good reader, she still didn't know much American history. I tried to read the history book by myself, but it was just too hard. *I'll have to wait a little longer to become a citizen.*

CHAPTER THREE – 1927

I kept thinking about what I should do about becoming a citizen, when a few months later something wonderful happened. I met a young man named Dave at a concert in Central Park. Soon we knew we wanted to get married. Since Dave was born in America, he knew a lot about American history. I thought that maybe after we were married, he would help me study to become a citizen.

"Of course, I'll help you, Clara," he assured me. "Every night after we are married, we'll read American history books together. It won't be long before you will be ready to take the citizenship test. You'll pass with flying colors!"

I wasn't sure what flying colors were, but I was very happy.

But after we got married, life was busy. I was working in the dress factory and when I came home at night, I had to shop, prepare dinner, clean the house, and do the laundry. I was just too tired to think about American history!

And then something else wonderful was going to happen. I would have a baby. Yes. I was so happy. And for a time, I stopped thinking about becoming a citizen.

CHAPTER FOUR – 1928 - 1933

In December, 1928, I had a beautiful daughter. Dave and I named her Evelyn. I stopped working in the dress factory, but I was busier than ever. I had to wash diapers, go shopping for food, and cook dinner when Dave came home from work. And I had to be sure to take Evelyn out every day for a walk so that she would have fresh air and be healthy.

I also made sure to speak only English to Evelyn so that she would be good at it when she went to school. Every once in a while I thought again about becoming a citizen, but who had time to learn American history with so much to do?

A few years later, I had another baby, a little boy, and we named him Bernie. Evelyn loved Bernie, and Bernie loved Evelyn and that was good. I was happy to have two lovely children and I stopped thinking altogether about becoming a citizen.

CHAPTER FIVE – 1938 – 1939

In 1938 all of us in America were hearing very bad news about a man named Adolf Hitler, a political leader in Germany. He was making speeches to large crowds, telling them that Germany would soon take over every country in Europe and maybe the world. He promised the German people that they would have the strongest army and the best guns and would be able to beat every enemy. Many immigrants in America were afraid of these speeches.

"What if there's a war in Europe?" people would say. "What if America has to fight Germany?" What if America decides to send its immigrants who are not citizens back to Europe?"

The last question made me shake. I could not sleep and lost my appetite. Could this really happen? What would happen to Evelyn and Bernie? They were citizens because they were born in America. And so was their father. But me? Could I really be sent back to Europe?

Now I knew I *had* to become a citizen, no matter how busy I was. I would fill out the documents called Naturalization Papers, or first papers. It would take a few more years till I would get my second papers and take the test. In the meantime I would study American history. But I would need help, a lot of help.

Evelyn was now in the fifth grade. I looked at her schoolbooks and saw one that was called *American History for Elementary School Students*. I opened it up to the chapter that said, "George Washington Becomes the First President." I could read all the words and understand almost everything! Suddenly I knew what I could do.

I asked Evelyn to sit down with me at the kitchen table.

"I have something to ask you, something very important for me and for you too."

Evelyn looked a little nervous. I could see the worry on her face. What could I possibly want her to do?

"Will you be my teacher?" I asked.

"What do you mean?"

"I want to become a citizen, and I need to learn American history. Will you let me read your history book with you?"

At first Evelyn wasn't sure what I meant.
"Why do you want to read *my* history
book?"

"Because the answers to all the questions on the citizenship test are in your book. And you can help me remember them because you're smart and know English."

I knew Evelyn would say yes. She always said yes when I asked for help in learning. I took her with me to the Naturalization Office, and we got a copy of some of the questions that might be on the test. First I had to be sure about the presidents. I knew that George Washington was the first president. I also knew that Franklin D. Roosevelt was the thirty-second president because he had been president since 1933 and the radio announcers would say, *Our thirty-second President, Franklin D. Roosevelt.* I could even name the vice president, who was John Nance Garner. I also knew Abraham Lincoln because he had freed the slaves. Everyone I knew thought he was wonderful.

And so we began our lessons together, which we had every night during the week. At my first lesson with Evelyn, I asked if Abraham Lincoln was the second president. Evelyn started to laugh, but then covered her mouth.

"What's so funny?" I asked.

"Mom, Lincoln was the sixteenth president."

I suddenly got very nervous. If Abraham Lincoln was the sixteenth president, would I have to know all the presidents who came before him? And what about all the presidents who came *after* him up to Roosevelt?

"Don't worry, Mom. They'll only ask about the famous presidents." I was relieved.

Then every night that Evelyn and I studied together, she would ask me two or three questions from the test, like "What do we call changes to the Constitution? What did the Declaration of Independence do? Who is the Commander-in-Chief of the Armed Forces?"

Many times I didn't even understand what the words meant. What is an amendment? What is a declaration?

But Evelyn was very patient and I was very proud of her because she always knew the answers. Even if I were to fail my test, at least Evelyn would pass her tests and get high marks from her teachers.

CHAPTER SIX – 1939 - 1941

In September, 1939, Hitler invaded Poland and World War II began. France and England declared war against Germany. In America, we hoped that we wouldn't have to go to war, but when Germany invaded Belgium and Holland in 1940, lots of Americans were very worried. France had to surrender to Germany, and every night England was getting bombed. It was a disaster.

I didn't think that I could be sent back to Europe anymore because of the war, but every day I checked the mail for my papers that would say I could come in for the citizenship test.

Then in February, 1941, I got the letter from the Naturalization Office telling me that I could take my citizenship test. My date for the test was in the middle of March. I had just four weeks left to study!

Evelyn, who was now in junior high school, knew a lot of American history. So that night after Evelyn finished her homework, she showed me how to answer the questions.

"This is a short answer test," she told me.

"What do you mean by *short* answer?"

"Well, first you read the question. Then you look at the four different answers that come after the question."

Evelyn opened her history book and turned to the back where there were tests she could take for practice.

"Look," she said. "Here is one you might get."

In what year was the Constitution written?

    a) 1776
    b) 1787
    c) 1876
    d) 1812

I almost fainted when I saw that question. "How can I know that?" I asked Evelyn. "I never went to school like you. I'll never pass, never."

Evelyn took my hand as if she were the mother and I was the child. "This is how you do it. My teachers told us how to take a short answer test. Look at the dates, Mom. Which one are you sure is *wrong*?"

I read each date. Then I took a breath and said, "1876."

"You're right! How did you know?"

I said, "That's too late. I think the Constitution happened in the 1700s."

"Great!" Evelyn said. "So which other date is wrong?"

That was easy now. "1812."

Evelyn smiled and squeezed my hand. "Here you go—just 50-50. What do you think? 1776 or 1787?"

I thought and thought. Then I remembered. July 4, 1776. That was not the Constitution. It was…it was…the Declaration.

"1787?"

Evelyn hugged me and I hugged her. "You're right, Mom. That's how you take a short answer test."

Evelyn then gave me more rules. "First, be certain to answer all the questions you're sure of, even if they come at the end of the test. Then at least you'll have *those* answers right. Then go to the questions like the one on the Constitution, where you know that two of the answers are wrong. Then you have a 50-50 chance. Think of why one of the questions is the wrong or right answer. Finally, answer all the questions that are left. You might just get some right."

"What would I do without you, Evelyn? What would I do without you?"

Then every night we studied. I wasn't sure if I wanted March to come fast and be over with or just not come at all. We went over all the questions that might come up:

- When was the Declaration of Independence written?

That's easy. 1776. I don't have to read the other answers.

- What are the first ten amendments to the Constitution called?

This is harder. No, it's not the Preamble. I never even heard that word. It can't be called the First Ten Amendments. Why would they ask such a silly question? It's not the Mayflower Compact, because that goes with the Pilgrims. "The Bill of Rights!!"

Evelyn clapped. "You're going to do it, Mom! You will do it."

Some nights I was tired and so was Evelyn. But during the whole year that we worked together, she never let me miss a lesson unless she had her own test to study for.

The night before the test, we decided not to study. I made a special dinner for all of us. I roasted a chicken with small potatoes and garlic. Then I made a special noodle dish that my family called *noodle kugel*. For a green vegetable I made some string beans with almonds.

On his way home from work, Dave stopped
at Sutter's Bakery in downtown New York
to pick up one of their extra delicious cakes
for our dessert. I thought, *If I don't pass
the citizenship test, at least my family will
remember this special dinner. And if I do pass
it...........*

On the morning of my test, Bernie and Evelyn went off to school and Dave went to work as usual. Everyone kissed me and wished me luck.

"Remember to answer the questions you know first, Mom," Evelyn reminded me, and then whispered, "I know you'll pass with flying colors."

My sister Sylvia came to get me and we both walked to the Naturalization Office a few blocks away. We didn't talk about the test because I thought that would make me more nervous.

I walked into the building, my head filled with words - *Declaration, Constitution, Amendments, Presidents, Bill of Rights*. What if I failed? I could take it again. But that would be terrible. And how would Evelyn feel? She had worked so hard to help me.

There seemed to be hundreds of people at the office, although maybe it was my imagination. A guard separated us into different rooms. It reminded me of how I felt when I came to America and we all went into the different rooms at Ellis Island. How could I be with so many people and feel so alone?

Then suddenly I saw my friend Filomena Domenica, whom I had met at night school. She was taking the test too. We had two or three minutes to talk.

"How are you?" I asked.

"Good. I'm married."

"Me too."

"I have two children, Tony and Angela."

"Me too. I mean I have Evelyn and Bernie. Well, good luck, Filomena. I know you'll pass."

"Good luck, Clara. You'll pass, I know you will."

We took our seats. Filomena Domenica was behind me, and I felt better just knowing she was there, although there was nothing she could do for me.

A man with a serious face gave out the papers, which he placed upside down on our desks.

"Don't turn your papers over till I tell you to. You will have thirty minutes to do ten questions. If you finish before the time is up, turn your paper over, raise your hand, and wait till I come over. After I take your paper, you may leave. Do not stay in the building. Good luck."

The test began. It was the first test I had taken since I left Europe, and that one wasn't even in English or about history. I kept hearing Evelyn's voice telling me how to do short answers—LOOK FOR THE ONES I KNEW FIRST. I chewed on my pencil for a minute and then began.

Question 3 - I knew that answer. Thirteen stripes on the American flag.

Question 6 - That was easy. Forty-eight states in the Union.

Question 9 - The date of Independence Day is July 4th. *Whew!*

I had only seven more to go, and I only needed to get seven out of ten right. I chewed my pencil again.

Question 1 - That's hard. What is the legislative branch? I know *Judicial* means *judges*. Then there is what the president does. He's the executive. Yes, yes. I remember. *Legislative* goes with *laws*. Both words begin with the letter L.

There were three more questions I had to get right. I looked at question 2: Who wrote The Star-Spangled Banner? I skipped it, as Evelyn told me to do when I didn't know.

I now had questions 4, 5, 7 8, and 10.

Please, let me know just four more answers, I thought.

Question 4 - What document freed the slaves? Not the Mayflower. No, not the Declaration. The Bill of Rights is in the Constitution. It must be answer C. I can't even say these words – Emanci..... Procl.....

But that's it! *Pick the best answer,* Evelyn had said.

Question 5 - Who is the Commander-in-Chief of the United States Armed Forces? I know that it's President Roosevelt, but it just says 'president.' That's it. Good.

Just questions 7 and 8. I could feel time was running out. I tried question 8 first, in case it was easy: Which president is called the "Father of Our Country?" It couldn't be Lincoln. He was the sixteenth president. And it wasn't Roosevelt. He was the thirty-second president. And I didn't know the names of the other choices of presidents except George Washington. That was it!

Back to question 7 - Which one of these states was one of the thirteen colonies? I closed my eyes and tried to see a map of the colonies along the Atlantic coast. Evelyn had told me to do this in case I was asked this question. I opened my eyes and read the choices:

a) Florida

b) Texas

c) North Carolina

d) California

Florida and North Carolina bordered the Atlantic Ocean. I chewed my pencil. Yes. It's North Carolina because there was also a *South* Carolina. I circled the letter C.

I had about five minutes left. I was up to question 10: Which amendment gave women the right to vote? That one was hard. But then I remembered that Evelyn told me that it was the Nineteenth Amendment and I would be able to vote when I became a citizen.

I went back to question 2 on the Star-Spangled Banner. I wanted to get it right in case one of my other answers was wrong. I did what Evelyn said, *Take a guess, just in case. Never leave it blank.* I circled the letter B and I can't even remember who it was.

The man with the serious face told us to
stop and turn our papers over. He then
collected all of them, never even smiling.
But then, why should he smile?

I walked out with Filomena Domenica,
and we hugged and wished each other luck
again. Filomena spoke good English now,
but still with a funny accent. It was like my
funny accent, only different.

The weeks of waiting were long. Every day
from April to May I checked the mailbox.
Evelyn stopped asking me because she could
tell from my face that there was no news.
June came and still no news. *Maybe only the
people who passed got news,* I thought. *Maybe
people who didn't pass just didn't get a letter.*

"You can take it again, Mom," Evelyn said one day in the middle of June. "Lots of people take it again and then pass. Three people in my class told me that their mother or father didn't pass the first time." I shook my head and bit my lip. I didn't want to cry in front of my own child.

I stopped going to the mailbox for a whole week. It was the end of June, and Evelyn was coming home early every day. "Give me the mailbox key," she'd say. "I'm going to get the mail. You can't let the box get stuffed." I knew she was right.

Evelyn ran out the door and went down in the elevator. I waited at the kitchen table trying to think about what to make for dinner. I would know right away if I had passed or hadn't. A big envelope would mean I passed and….. Evelyn was back… smiling.

A big envelope. She had a big envelope.

We opened it up and there it was:

THE UNITED STATES OF AMERICA

CERTIFICATE OF NATURALIZATION

CLARA BIERMAN

JUNE 22, 1941

We hugged, we danced, we shouted. I was a citizen of the United States of America! I could vote. I could *not* be sent back to Europe. I had learned how to take a short answer test.

In a few weeks, I would take something called an *Oath of Allegiance,* which meant that I promised to defend the Constitution. My whole family would come to hear me and other new Americans say these words. I was so happy.

That night I made a delicious supper for Dave, Evelyn, and Bernie. Everyone was proud of me, especially Evelyn. And best of all, I was proud of Evelyn.

* * *

STUDY GUIDE FOR
CLARA BECOMES A CITIZEN

In this section of the book you will find:
- Clara's test to become a citizen, which you can take to test your knowledge of American history.
- Headlines from 1920 to 1941 that tell events of those years, and questions you can think about and answer.
- Changes in the laws from 1790 to 1965 that concern requirements for becoming a citizen and voting.

Here is Clara's short answer test to become a citizen of the United States. How many questions can you get right? Go back to the story to check your answers.

1) The United States has three branches of government. What is the role of the Legislative Branch?
2) Who wrote the Star-Spangled Banner?
3) How many stripes are on the American flag?
4) What document gave freedom to the slaves?
5) Who was the Commander-in-Chief of the United States Armed Forces in 1941? And who is Commander-in-Chief now?
6) How many states were there in the Union in 1941? And how many are there now?

7) Which one of these states was part of the original thirteen colonies?
   a) Florida
   b) Texas
   c) North Carolina
   d) California
8) Which president is called "The Father of Our Country?"
9) What historic even do we celebrate on July 4th?
10) Which amendment gave women the right to vote?

* * *

Oath of Allegiance for Naturalized Citizens

I hereby declare, on oath, that I absolutely and entirely renounce and abjure all allegiance and fidelity to any foreign prince, potentate, state, or sovereignty of whom or which I have heretofore been a subject or citizen; that I will support and defend the Constitution and laws of the United States of America against all enemies, foreign and domestic; that I will bear true faith and allegiance to the same; that I will bear arms on behalf of the United States when required by the law; that I will perform noncombatant service in the Armed Forces of the United States when required by the law; that I will perform work of national importance under civilian direction when required by the law; and that I take this obligation freely without any mental reservation or purpose of evasion, so help me God.

Headlines of 1920

WARREN G. HARDING ELECTED PRESIDENT

Babe Ruth Traded by the Boston Red Sox
to the New York Yankees for $125,000

First Game of Negro National League
Baseball Played in Indianapolis

Nineteenth Amendment Passed, Giving Women Right to Vote

First Radio Broadcast a Success

* * *

Headlines of 1925 and 1926

Minnesota Mining & Manufacturing
Company has New Product Named
"Scotch Tape"

Tennessee Entrepreneur Frieda Carter Designs Miniature Golf Course at Fairyland Inn Resort

Gertrude Ederle, 19, Becomes First
Woman to Swim English Channel

Toastmaster, First Pop-Up Toaster, Browns
Both Slices of Bread at Same Time!

* * *

Headlines of 1927

President Roosevelt Founds Warm
Springs Foundation Center for
Victims of Poliomyelitis

Transatlantic Telephone Service Begins
Between London and New York

New Invention Named "Television" is
Unveiled at Bell Telephone Laboratories

First Talking Movie—"The Jazz Singer"—
Brings Crowds to Theaters

* * *

Headlines of 1928-1933

1928: Commander Richard E. Byrd Mounts
Huge Expedition to Antarctica

1929: FRANK H. FLEER, INVENTOR OF DUBBLE BUBBLE GUM, TEACHES SALES FORCE TO BLOW BUBBLES

1930: Astronomer Clyde Thombaugh
Discovers New Planet, Names it "Pluto"

1931: New York's 102-Story Empire State Building Opens with Formal Ceremonies

1932: POSTAL RATE GOES FROM 2¢ TO 3¢

1933: Adolf Hitler Becomes Dictator
of the German Reich

* * *

Headlines of 1938

Hitler Marches into Czechoslovakia,
Taking Over Sudentenland,
16,000 Square Miles of Territory

Hitler Annexes Austria, Deprives Jews
of Civil Rights

Hitler Orders Arrest of Thousands of
Gypsies (Roma), Homosexuals, and
Disabled Adults

Hitler Orders all Non-Jews to Destroy
Jewish Homes and Businesses

* * *

Headlines of 1939

Hitler's Troops and Tanks Invade Poland,
Beginning World War II

HITLER SIGNS NON-AGGRESSION PACT WITH SOVIET LEADER JOSEF STALIN

France Evacuates 16,000 Children,
Fearing German Invasion

**Two Torpedoes from German
Submarine Hit British Escort Carrier
HMS Courageous, Killing 576 Men**

* * *

Headlines of 1940

German Troops Seize Oslo and Bergen
Occupation of Norway;
German Troops Occupy Denmark

Paris Falls to Germans as Fighting Rages Along the Maginot Line

"I Have Nothing to Offer but Blood, Toil,
Tears, and Sweat," New Prime Minister
Winston Churchill Tells
House of Commons

* * *

Headlines of 1941

Major Weapon Against Infectious
Diseases, Named Penicillin, Developed
by Howard Florey

**President Roosevelt Calls for a World
of "Four Freedoms" - Freedom of
Speech and Expression, Freedom
of Religion, Freedom from Want,
Freedom from Fear**

Japanese Forces Attack Pearl Harbor,
Destroying 200 United States Planes and
Killing 2,344 Men

* * *

A Short History of Citizens and Voting in the United States

When the United States Constitution was ratified (agreed upon and signed) in 1787, only white males born in the United States were citizens. But only white males who *owned property* had the right to vote. Little by little, different states allowed white males without property to vote. But it was not until 1850 that *all* white males born in the United States, with or without property, had the right to vote.

* * *

The First Naturalization Act—Becoming a Citizen of the United States

On March 26, 1790, Congress passed a law that would allow people who were not born in the United States to become citizens. The people granted this right had to be free (not a slave), white, adult, and male or female, and have resided in the United States for two years. They had to prove to a federal or state court that they were of good moral character and they had to pledge their allegiance to the Constitution. If the parents were granted citizenship, their children under twenty-one years of age would automatically become citizens. In 1795, the period of residence for becoming a citizen was changed from two years to five years. However, only males over twenty-one years of age could vote, and in many states owning property was still required.

* * *

The Fourteenth Amendment to the Constitution

On July 28, 1868, three years after the Civil War, the XIV Amendment to the Constitution stated, "All persons born or naturalized in the United States…are citizens of the United States…." This amendment made African-Americans citizens, but did

not give them the right to vote. Nor could
women, American Indians, Chinese, or
Japanese people vote.

* * *

The Fifteenth Amendment to
the Constitution

This amendment, passed in 1870, gave
African-American men the right to vote by
declaring that the "right of citizens of the
United States to vote shall not be denied
or abridged by the United States or by any
state on account of race, color, or previous
condition of servitude." Although ratified on
February 3, 1870, African Americans were
often unable to vote because in many states
they were required to pay poll taxes (money
to vote) or pass literacy (reading) tests that
were difficult and not required of white
people. Not until the passage of the Voting
Rights Act of 1965 could the majority of
African Americans vote.

* * *

Restrictions on Naturalization and Voting

Naturalization rights for Chinese, Japanese, and other Asian peoples were not included, even though the Fifteenth Amendment stated that race and color would not be a restriction.

In 1868, the United States government allowed Chinese people to immigrate to the United States, but did not give them the right of naturalization (becoming citizens). In 1943, because China was a wartime ally in the fight against Japan in the Second World War, Congress granted naturalization rights to foreign-born Chinese.

The issue of citizenship for Japanese immigrants was decided by the 1922 Supreme Court, which declared that Japanese immigrants and other people from Asia were not eligible for American citizenship. Only immigrants from the Philippines, which at that time was under the United States' control, could apply for naturalization.

* * *

The Nineteenth Amendment to the Constitution

On August 18, 1920, the Nineteenth Amendment gave women the right to vote, stating, "The right of citizens of the United States to vote shall not be denied or abridged by the United States or by any state on account of sex." This amendment took many years to pass and the work of many women and men who kept urging Congress to grant full citizenship rights not only to males, but to females who were either born in the United States or naturalized.

* * *

The Immigration Act of 1965

In 1965, President Lyndon Johnson signed a bill that dramatically changed the method by which immigrants were admitted to America. This bill was the Immigration Act of 1965, allowing people from many countries (including Asian and African countries) to enter the United States, apply for citizenship, and vote. Now all American citizens, regardless of gender, race, or country of birth, are eligible to vote after their eighteenth birthday.